apostrophe

acknowledgements:

some of these poems have already been published, or accepted for publication, in the following periodicals

Borderlines, Envoi, Orbis, Pennine Platform, Poetry Cornwall, Poetry Monthly

apostrophe
combe

Published by the boho press 2003

2 4 6 8 10 9 7 5 3 1

First published in Great Britain in 2003 by
The boho press
An Imprint of KMS Ltd
PO Box 109,
Portishead, Bristol. BS20 7ZJ

www.bohopress.co.uk

A CIP catalogue record for this book is available from the British Library

ISBN 1-904781-02-0

Glossy prints of any of the photographs here can be obtained by contacting Gemma Dart - gemmadart@hotmail.com

introductin

The original intention of this project was to make a photographic and written record of this one place, the manner conversational, thoughts arising from observations and incidents.

So far as form goes, I took as a starting point the poetry of Japan's Heian period (794-1185), when the predominate form was a sedoka sandwiched between two blocks of prose, and whose principal purpose was a declaration of the author's love. Here, however, there are very few love poems. But, having decided on the form, I then let the material dictate its presentation.

In the writing, in the taking and selecting of photographs, the overall thrust was to attempt to create a sense of place and time; that is of the past up to the moment of the writing, up to the moment of photographing. And then - with the words on the page, with the photographs - to create something other, where everyone's experience of the book, as with the place, will be different.

Sam Smith

Table of Contents

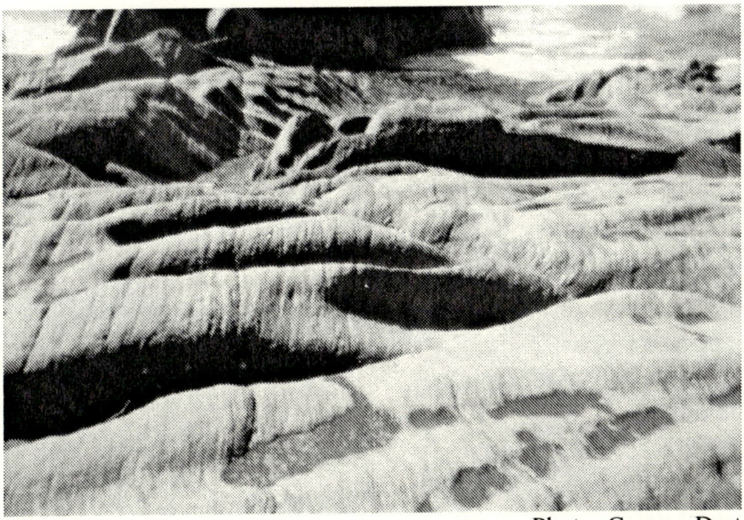

Photo: Gemma Dart

Here

To belong here,
but not to be owned,
we deny
the false identities of place
and history.
We, here, are not
where we came from.
Nor are we, here,
where we have arrived.
We, here, don't believe
what this local council says,
let alone
government mouthpieces.
Here,
not of a nation,
not of a people,
uncertain even
of here's name, here's spelling,
we call here
'apostrophe combe.'

Apostrophe Combe

Slant-stacked, unquarried, these slate cliffs are a wafered ice cake that has been snapped, then pushed together, refrozen and snapped again. Within stratas of slate are stratas of slate where water can penetrate. Through other stratas of black slate white and pink quartz has been dribbled and veined. On beach stumps this quartz is last to be eroded, becomes a globular warty mass, a dirty icing, no more picturesque than fire-melted plastic.

Above the lustrous blue
of a shale-silted sea,
over path-scarred heathland,
goes the flame-flicker rotation
of three brown butterflies.

Could as easily hate this place as love it. Arrive on a wet day, gusts from every which way flicking rain into your face, walk over/through drain surge and gurgle; and it will feel relentless, this ever-blowing wind, the wet that gets into everything. All that you will see of the grey sea is it roiling white around black rocks, misshapen balls of its khaki spume flying over the gulls sitting out the storm on the putting green. A sustained blast of wind will seem to hold down any house you are in. Only, on its cessation, for the house to balloon out as if to explode. Except that this time it doesn't. And you await the next blast.

12 – apostrophe combe – Sam Smith, Gemma Dart and Neil Carter

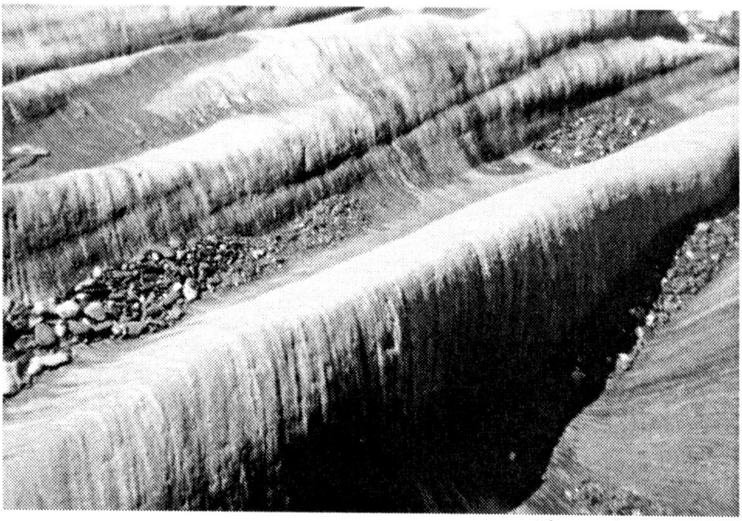

Photo: Gemma Dart

to Here

Slate beds got folded, thrust upward by tectonic drift and grind, folded and thrust again. Water and ice then cut a trough miles wide, left the folded strata exposed on cliffs' sides. Along one plate's edge a granite obtrusion bubbled up through the sea, became a mica-flecked island at the channel's mouth, on today's horizon a thickened charcoal line.

> At the base of a bracken cleft, summer-green
> winter-brown, on a shrapnel beach of frost-
> exploded shale, sits a forty ton block
> of Scottish rock, that floated here within
> the pale blue light
>   of a frozen ocean's moving ice.

In straight-backed ranks, front rows kneeling, triangular rocks await the sea's attack. And fail. The cliff's warped ply of slate and shale shows always fresh signs of collapse. This day gobs of spume come flying up and go rolling on over green pastures. Massed thorns rattle back at these insistent Westerlies, allow one-stemmed foxgloves a little height in their lee.

Spirit of No-Place

Made remote by the bleak uplands of Exmoor behind, tide race of the Bristol Channel before, these conjunctions and disjunctions of land and sea are difficult to reach, rather than inaccessible. Most of other men's history, nevertheless, has passed us by. The Romans rowed on past to Wales, square-rigged slavers sailed on up to Bristol, Athelstan's men marched south of here against the Cornish; and from here, outside air-raid shelters, we watched Swansea burn.

In this no-place of misfits and miscreants
men passed in summer's street smell of stale
armpit sweat. Wet winter queues are rank
with unwashed clothes. All-weather drunks
sit in pairs on corner benches,
a single bottle between them.

The Dumnonii were 'people of the land.' Here, on this north-facing coast, they were not quite, being also of the sea and thus having as much in common with Celtic harbour folk. Here Irish legend, Welsh and Dumnonii myth wind about each other like belt buckles. Even now the clearest radio stations are Welsh.

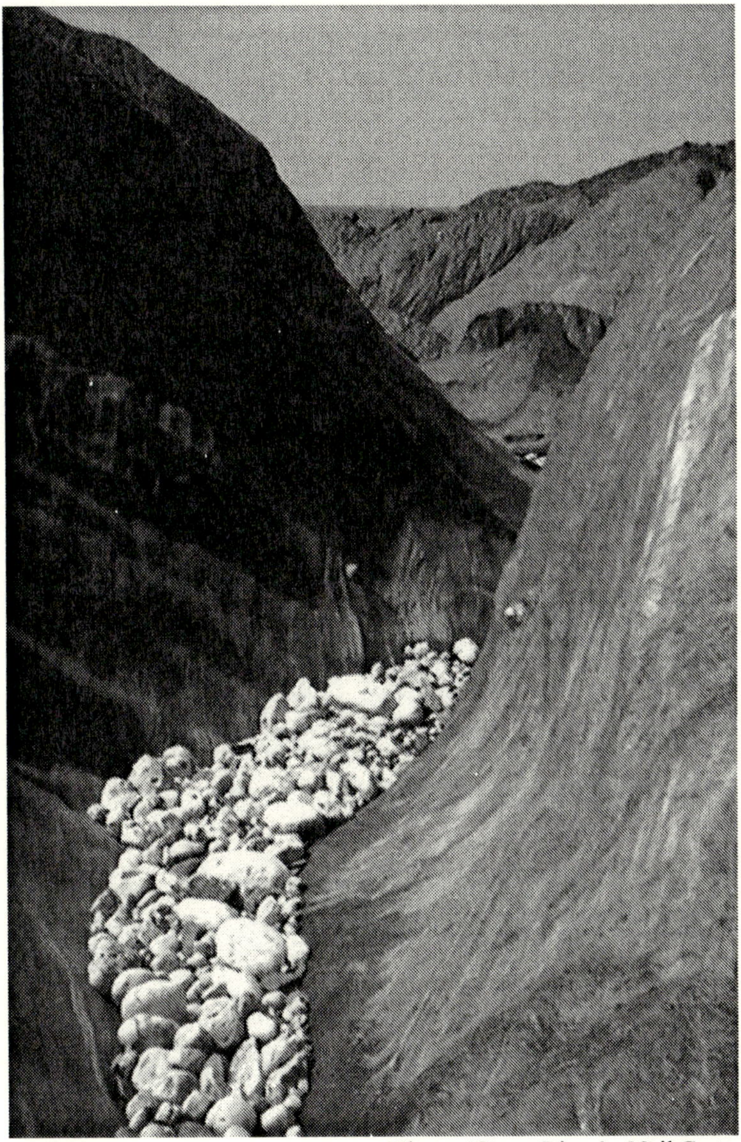

Photo: 'Stone River' - Neil Carter

'combe haiku

calm day sea shimmer:
one wet black pebble, hand-turned,
parcel-tied with quartz

Negatives

Not a scene,
nor a portion; not a puzzling
perspective of a part
of a moment:

recorded with a camera flash,
it becomes not
the memory of the moment,
(may not even resemble the moment:)

the photograph instead
becomes an image,
an event in itself
every time that (fading)
it is shown

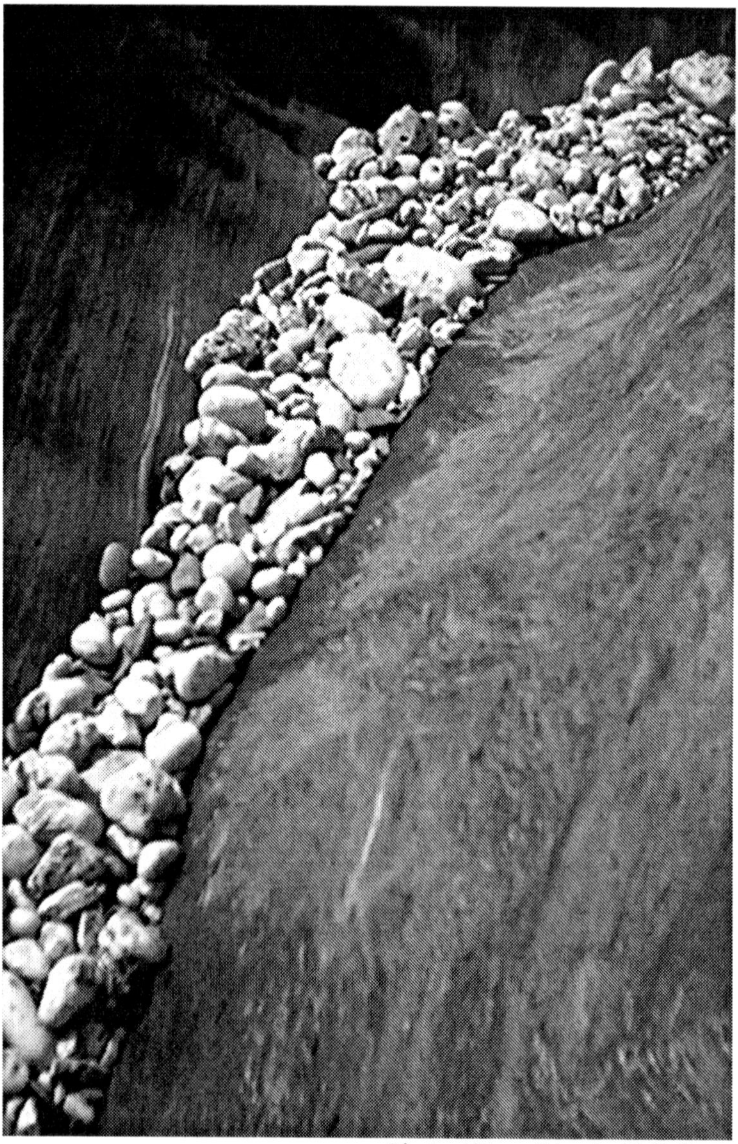

Photo: 'Stone River' - Neil Carter

'combe haiku

on clifftops, above
a fluffed, wind-teased sea, crickets
persist in their noise

History 1

Feral pigeons keep low, out of the falcon's line of sight. We Dumnonii never were a fighting force. A tribe that doubts itself, each part distrustful and contemptuous of all its other parts, our hatred for each other is greater than for any of our alleged enemies. Truth be told we're more likely to do a deal with an 'enemy' just to do a neighbour down. So we traded with Egyptians, Byzantines and Turks; watched Romans make a landing beyond Great Hangman. Further south every hilltop had a fort. What did we have here? Hills aplenty, but few of us to rule, and fewer to be afeared of. Most we feared was a plague of fairies and elves. Even when church first came with its charity and its stories, and we said yes, we still made our offerings into the earth and into the rock. Only when church demanded tithes did we of the Dumnonii say no. Then we went briefly back to a lore beyond true recall, a sense of something meaningful further on, that took the curious up to the stones. But church, once started, wouldn't stop, had fighting Norsemen to disprove. And very soon, selling each other out, we of the Dumnonii had our thoughts locked to the ground, bound to hamlet and village by the round of our toils, minds dead-ended by gospels, spirits gripped by new superstitions, like pebbles by the holdfast roots of oarweed.

History 2

Us pagan Pardoes, late of the Dumnonii, paid no mind to incomers. Even when they took our old spirits and called them saint this and saint that. Them that could be bothered still went up the stones. And twas the same we asked favours of, prayed to - for good fortune, good health, good crops, good catch and safe journeys. And, sometimes, it worked. When they built a church they let us hold market there. Brought troubles with them too, mind you. Norsemen took against the new. Hard, though, with a westerly of any strength, to make harbour here. And it blows more often than it don't. Most coasters got to be warped in. So the Norsemen made softer landings further on up, stayed there years and more. When wind and tide allowed, they paid us a crafty visit or two, took a few stock. Got blamed anyway. We had our own feuds of course, brawled once good'n proper at market. That got us kicked out of churchyard. Norsemen got kicked out too. All got serious after that. Though, seemed to more than a few of us, clergy was keener on raising tithes than holding services. They'm still here. Just. Harbour chapel, which wasn't a chapel, and is a chapel no more, was named after Nicholas, patron saint of sailors and scholars. Scholars here.... there's a thought.

22 – apostrophe combe – Sam Smith, Gemma Dart and Neil Carter

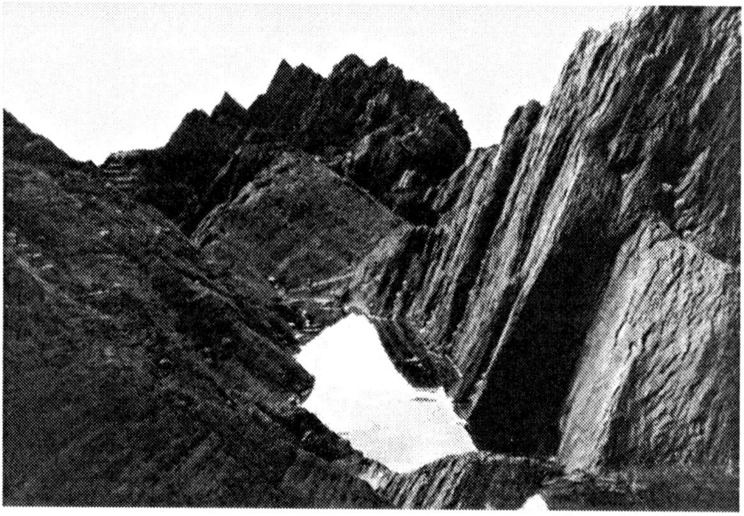

Photo: Neil Carter

'combe tanka

O giver of salt!
Before this mineral & metal mix,
cross-hatching of ripples
the shore is a jaggedly barren
science fiction rockscape.

'Combe Pardoes

Head down Pardoes,
we never did touch
forelocks, but nor
do we fight, make
angry gestures. We live
inside our own lives, have
no sense of industry,
just of getting by.
We avoid taxes like
the plague. Wages
miss us too, though
we pay our dues
in other ways.

Bird shadow over
bald green hillsides,
one sail coasters
with their crew of two:
most the world
passes by us Pardoes,
late of the Dumnonii,
misfits and
miscreants all.

Church poor Pardoes,
pick oakum
from old ropes,
get paid in tobacco.
Histories we've got, if not
names. But we're not
local, nor are we
characters, just
uncouth. You wouldn't
want some of our breed
for neighbours.

Expectation of big profits
got too many houses
built here. Now it's only
us halophyte Pardoes,
with our lumpy
red potato faces,
who can live on little,
who stay.

And us Pardoes,
used to gullmockery,
take no offence
at what stops off:
Pardoe women
have always been
obliging. And still we
find our way here,
Pardoes new, for who
the odd makes sense
and the even
doesn't add up.

26 – apostrophe combe – Sam Smith, Gemma Dart and Neil Carter

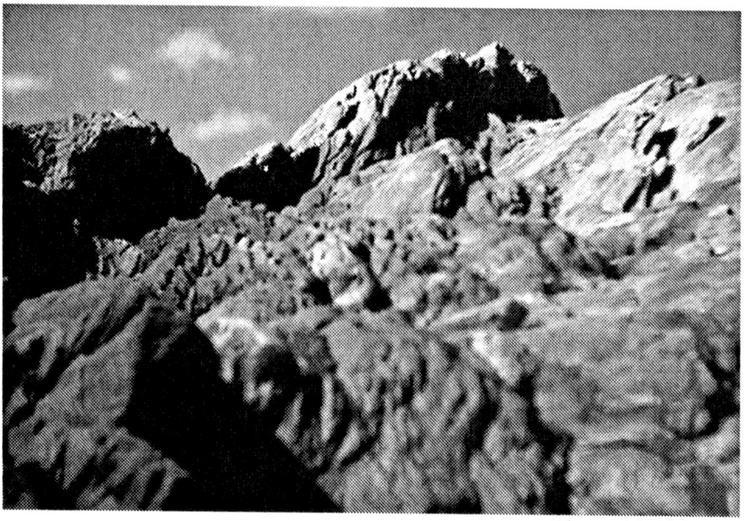

Photo: Neil Carter

'combe haiku

fossils deform
and recrystallise: Earth
has no solidity

28 – apostrophe combe – Sam Smith, Gemma Dart and Neil Carter

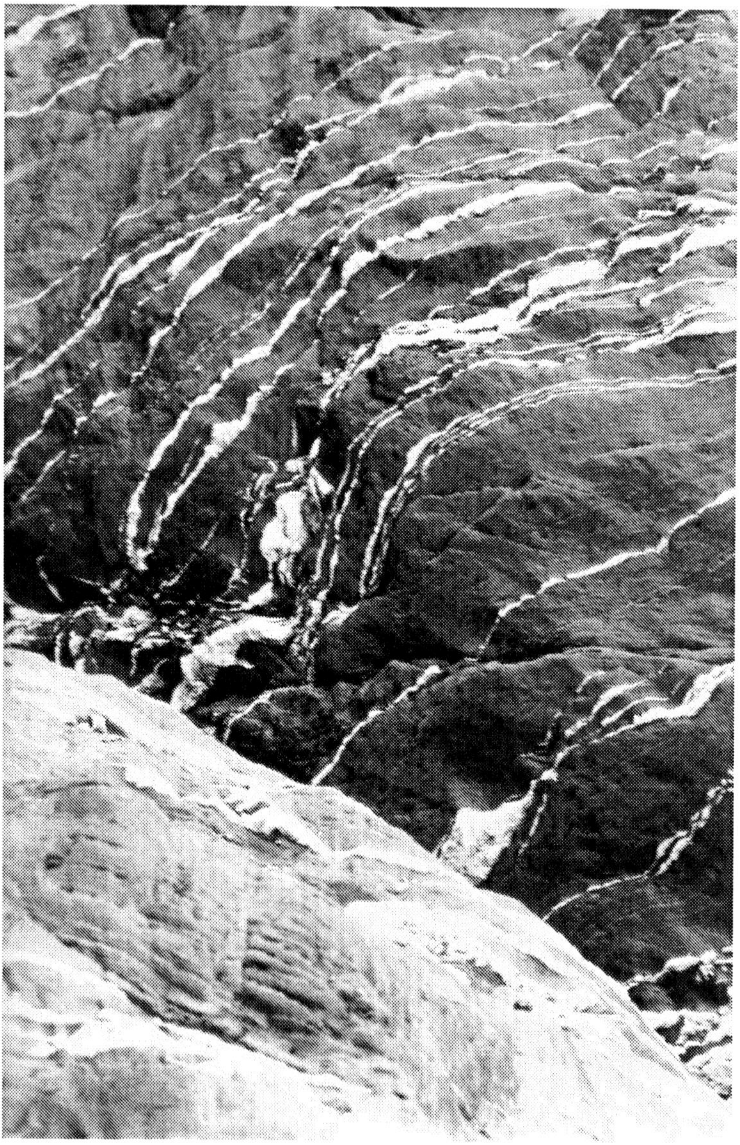

Photo: Neil Carter

Us Dumnonii

Remote, but not isolated, Dumnonia once encompassed the whole of Kernow and Breton. Despite its domain its King Constantine was still referred to as the '*unclean whelp of the lioness of Dumnonia.*' George Eliot said that 'combe was '*not a favourable place for delicate people.*' Charles Kingsley too urged 'combe council '*to tighten up their sanitary slackness.*'

On a gorse forest floor
of brown needles, sunbeams
spiking the green canopy, in
among the twisted, bristled
stems, a sinewy viper, in
coils of brown
          and black, basks.

The new Dumnonii are still a tainted, still a painted people. But, while the Yakuza may have as many tattoos, this western peninsula will never have any large scale organised crime. Here we are still too eager to grass on our neighbours, to steal from our work colleagues; and, to be a meaningful thief, you have to despise those you are stealing from. Winters, here, there's no-one else but us.

30 – apostrophe combe – Sam Smith, Gemma Dart and Neil Carter

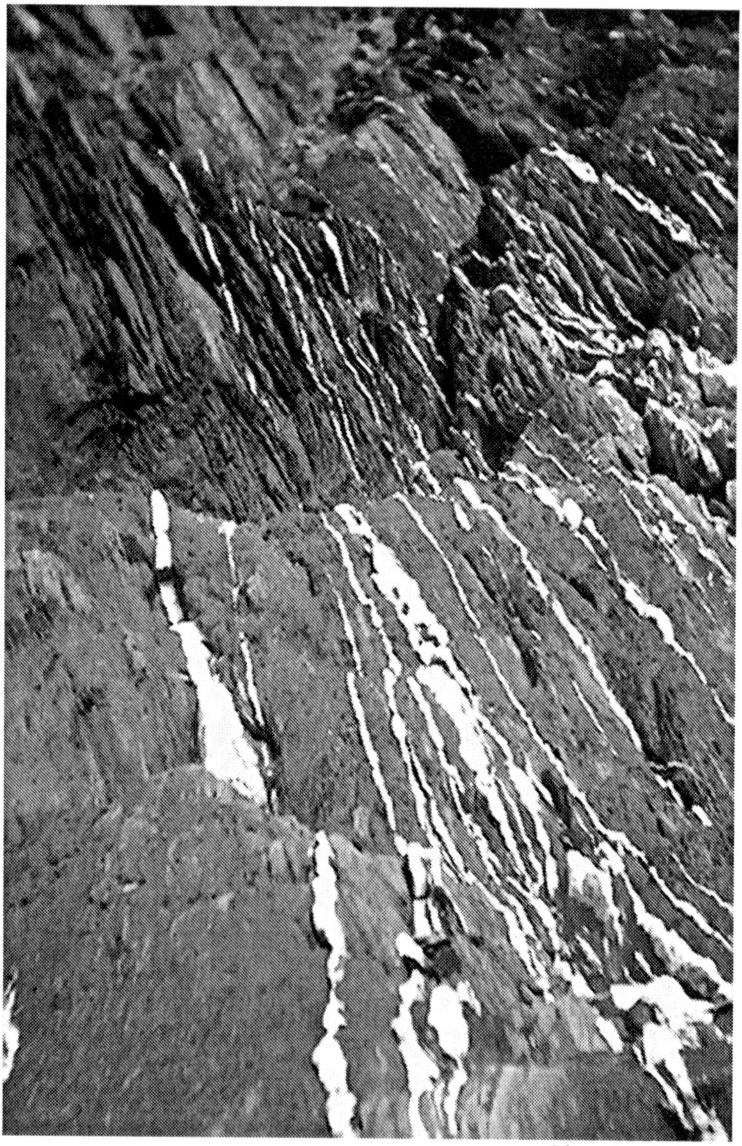

Photo: Neil Carter

'combe haiku

a cross-hatched sea
carves white light into shifting
cobalt-edged triangles

"Like all ideal things,
they are moving
on the very edge
of Death."
Frederico Garcia Lorca

Romantic Love

Each season, from the cliff's sloping strata, a new slab, a new parallelogram of rock, will slide off. Other cliffs are precarious tower upon tower of gamblers' chips. Rock turret ravens make their nests here. Pairs of quick, grey-backed peregrines too. The echoes of kittiwake cries make only seagull sense. Gleaming at cliff's base are banded mounds of brown serrated wrack; lifted by seawater, going gold. On this clifftop edge a cushion matting of moorland grass.

She stands on the precipice of love.
The sea is photograph still
and speaking, on beach frills, with the soft tongues
of wavelets. Or, is it, a sexual tasting? His warmth
to her has made him beautiful. To another
he is just another. She is smiling.

From before Tristram, the Irish too came here. And did Tristram, with Iseult, on those long-flecked swells of autumn, love-sick, look away to these cliffs, to this once-escarpment? To the straggling homeward march of ragged clouds along this green horizon? Out of faces that were masks, did Tristram and Iseult look to one another, an incision of eyes by eyes, with knowledge of a future as brutal to them as rocks to a mariner?

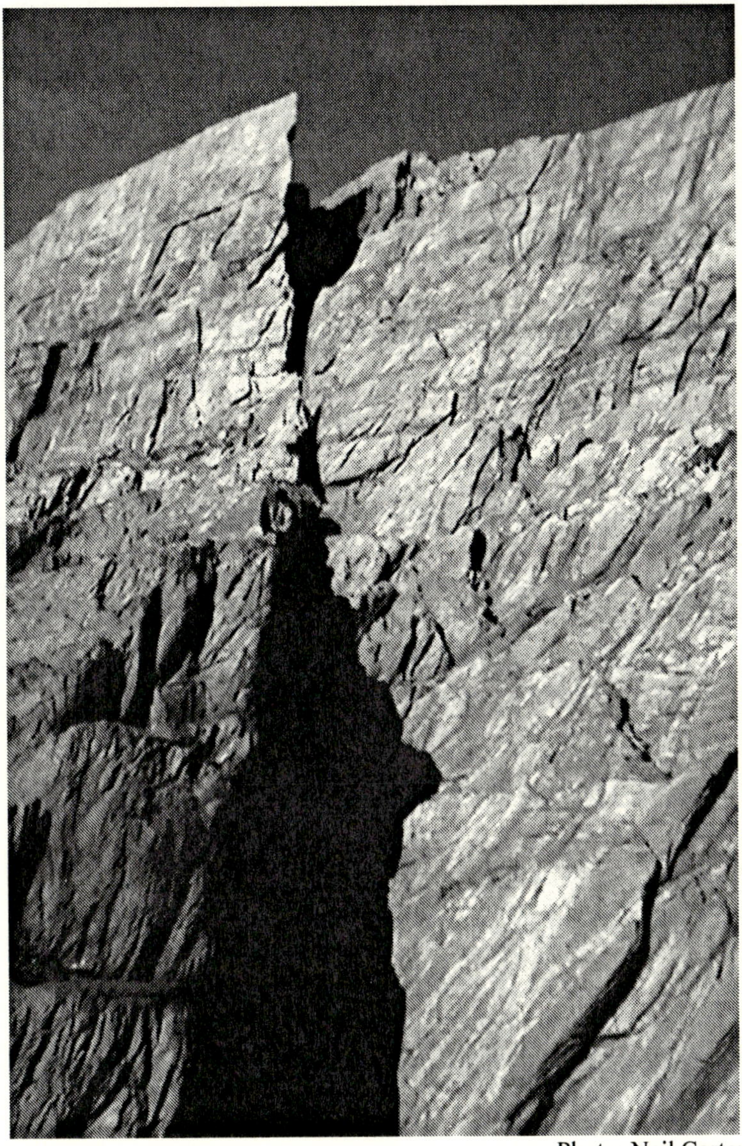

Photo: Neil Carter

"Solitude either developes the mental powers or renders men dull and vicious."
Victor Hugo

Between Void and Void

On the edge of the universe, on the outside of this planet, on this salt-tainted rim of unstable rock, on this ever-beginning and absolute end of the world's one sea, in a green combe above a harbour, property speculators once erected cliffs and ledges, made a nesting colony for gulls.

A place/No place, here is as uncertain as
its name. In the practice of their geometry,
gulls inspect the ever new, cove after cove,
circle after circle. Becoming concentric,
thoughts too begin to overlap, to lack
the substance and singleness of easy
expression. Gulls, standing, draw sound
from between their legs, straighten
their tubular gullets and blare out,
"True!" "True!" But it's a grievous truth,
the temporary condition of all our lives.

For the jackdaws are chimneypots of different shapes and sizes. Black fledglings emerge to cautiously walk the tiled roof crests. Fluffy brown gull chicks run on long legs along the flat roof tops, stop and flap their stubby wings. Incoming parent gulls inflate their throats to bleat and squeal down the blue spaces between derelict buildings.

'combe tanka

Rock solidity of
undulating slate strata is as thin
and dense as strands of hair.
Blue-grey horizon clouds follow
the contours of the darker hills.

36 – apostrophe combe – Sam Smith, Gemma Dart and Neil Carter

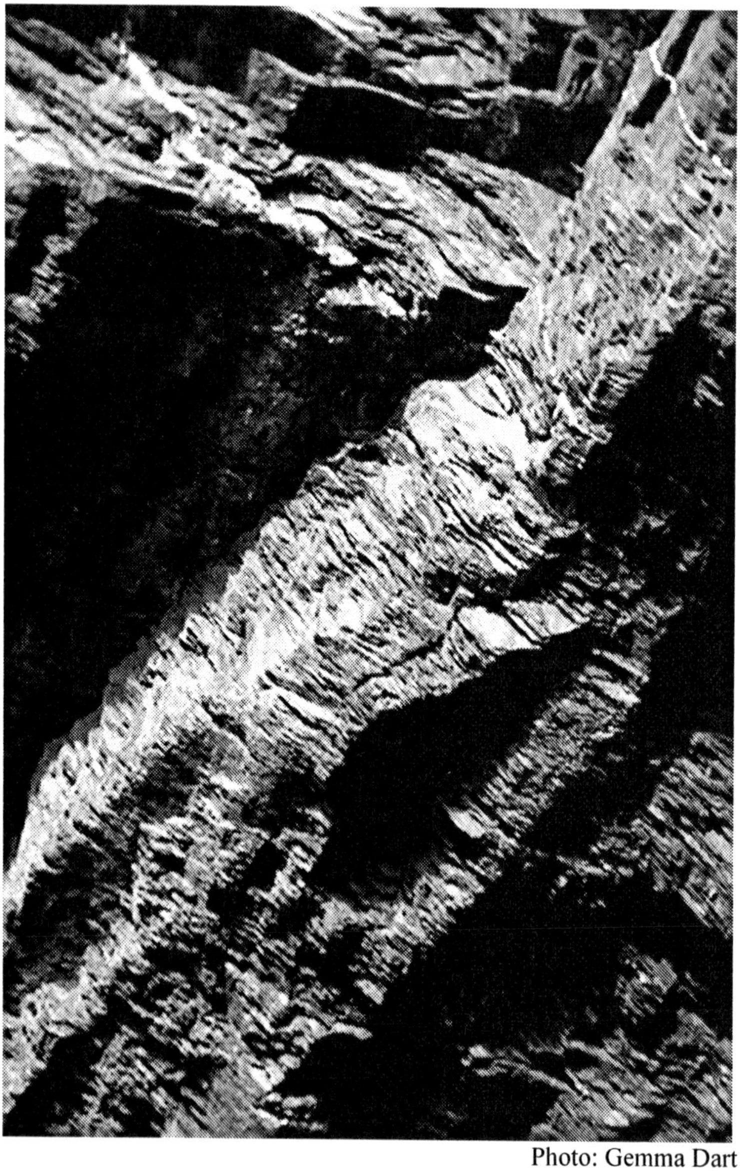

Photo: Gemma Dart

'combe haiku

a stiff-legged country
girl, market tat enclothing
her body's smells

Bloody Meadow

Civil war requires more than
native cunning to live beyond.

We, now, know of the past
only what has survived.
We, now, know of its context
only via what has been
transmitted and/or guessed at.

An archeological rumour, the once castle has no precise location. One surmised hill a probable vantage point; although any ruins were soon eroded, rubble taken and compacted into tracks and paths.

With the castle standing, we townsfolk
chose our time and swopped sides,
or took turns to surrender.
Like all grand politics, we knew that
the simplicities of war's outcome
would have no everyday impact on us:
the poor would stay poor, the rich get
richer; and we pressed soldiers,
of no importance to anyone but us, we
would not be bothered by the self-made
good and great again. Here, each man
and woman, a nation unto themself,
we looked to see which way the wind
was blowing, took sides, swapped sides,
marched loudly in opposite directions...
Until...

until in the flat meadow between the two
brooks, where summer upon summer
nesting rails creaked like donkey baskets,
there, trapped face to face, men and women
found themselves - the dank smells of marsh
rising around them - with no option but
to charge at their fellow townsfolk.
With earnest captains shouting, pikes being
brandished, individual survival saw
spiked sedges reddened that day.
Thereafter
Bloody Meadow it became. The rails
once again cracked the dusk, we
townsfolk having long retreated
back into ourselves.

History Is Always An Invention

Right and wrong come to depend on which direction you're looking, where you're coming from. Victorian trippers here made rock and sea adventures out of the ordinary that, repeated, was work for those that lived beside this sea, their hands swelling out to meet the wet and cold, ropes tight as iron and slippery as oil. The skin, engorged, split, cracks opening deep into the crimson flesh, salted fresh to pain, the pain ignored, and salted fresh again.

Reality and
hallucination
mixed,
creeping cold
as sea-mist,
each leaf-hanging drip
becomes a point of light,
every horizontal surface
black with
coalesced wet,
or glazed
with luminescence.

Charred gorse stalks
are snakes
arrested mid-dance,
stopped by
the sudden red
of woody nightshade.

Day-trippers now, consumer suspicious, sceptics and fault-finders all - with the weather if not prices and seaside practices - but still they are conditioned by a thousand photos to think breaking waves, white spray rising above black rocks, beautiful. As for the local misfits and miscreants, histories more supposed than known, some manifest as stumbling dreamers, others as louts. They are as prone. From all places, of all kinds, they are yet mostly bigots, are bringing their children up to be bigots. Butchers here fly the Union Jack.

42 – apostrophe combe – Sam Smith, Gemma Dart and Neil Carter

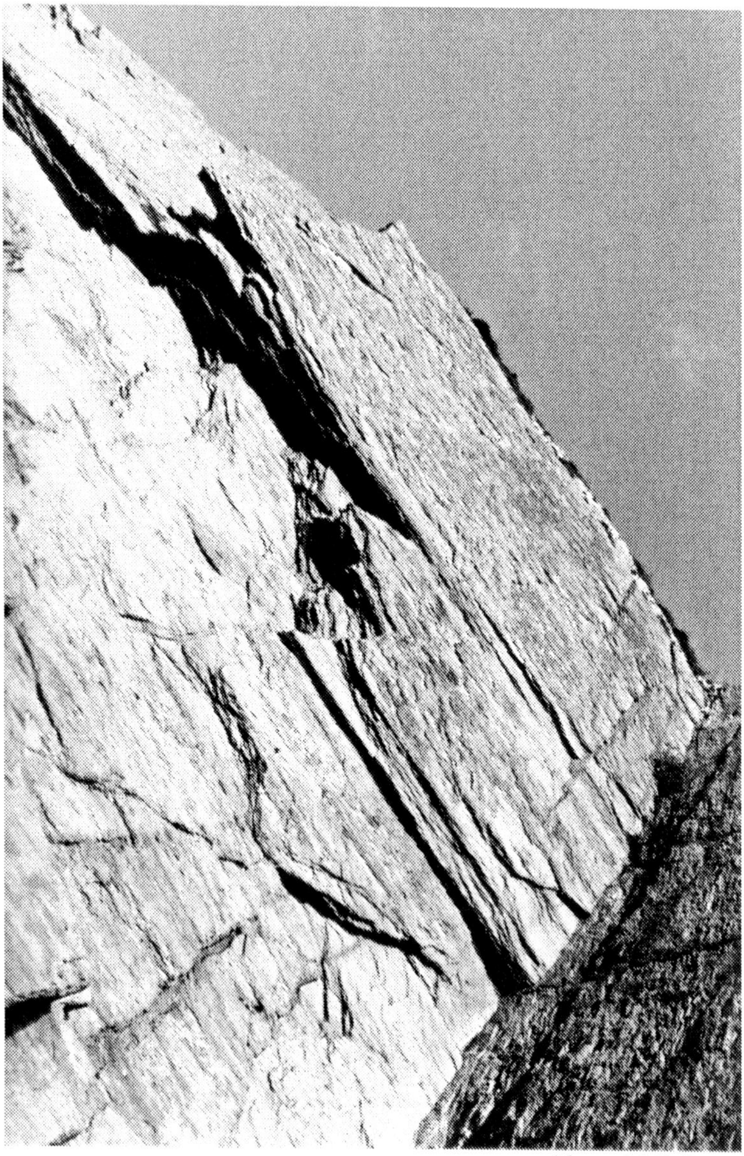

Photo: Neil Carter

tenuous

After the creation, and then the metamorphosis
of rock,
came the sea's chaos of molecules. In yet
another tectonic episode, fossils were deformed
and recrystallised.
Now land's bulk sits behind slanted rocket banks
of spiked rocks - aimed at the far North. To the South
the swingboat
strata of the cliffs is mimicked in the swoop of the fields
as they rise to the yellow moors. Above the caves'
crude architecture
of skew-whiff slate, walks have been sawn out of
the tooth-scarred rock. Buildings, of baked white brick,
sit vertically
on this tip-tilted rock. And here we people are,
between stone and stone, in this brief, dislocated
interval, that is
our one life. Gorse reclaims the steep green pastures.
Angled rocks push up through grass. Turf holds onto
clifftops as rock
separates from rock and slips away towards the sea.

'combe haiku

among asteroid and
moonscapes, tidepool reflections
carve blue triangles

Another History

The spiked rocks, way down below,
are the brown crystallising
solutions of a far too
blue sea. She stood here, haunted
by her own compulsion,
the world behind and beyond,
every imagined step
away offering up
unknowable alternatives.

Here, right here, in this wet town
of wet winds, in a damp room
populated by snails, teased
by water noises, ignoring
the love murmurs of a
chimney gull,
Mary Ann Evans came upon
the power of untruth, took
a male name and started
telling fictions.

46 – apostrophe combe – Sam Smith, Gemma Dart and Neil Carter

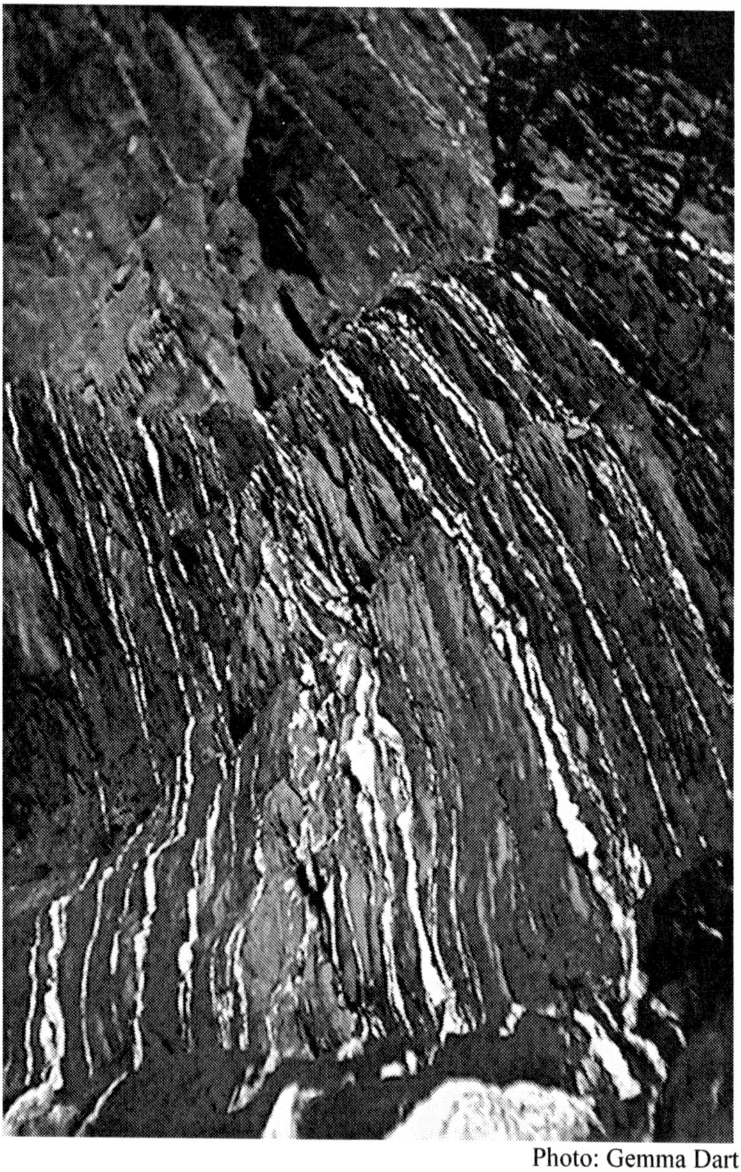

Photo: Gemma Dart

'combe haiku

White sails are adrift
in a sky of mist: we are exhibits
in a museum town

48 – apostrophe combe – Sam Smith, Gemma Dart and Neil Carter

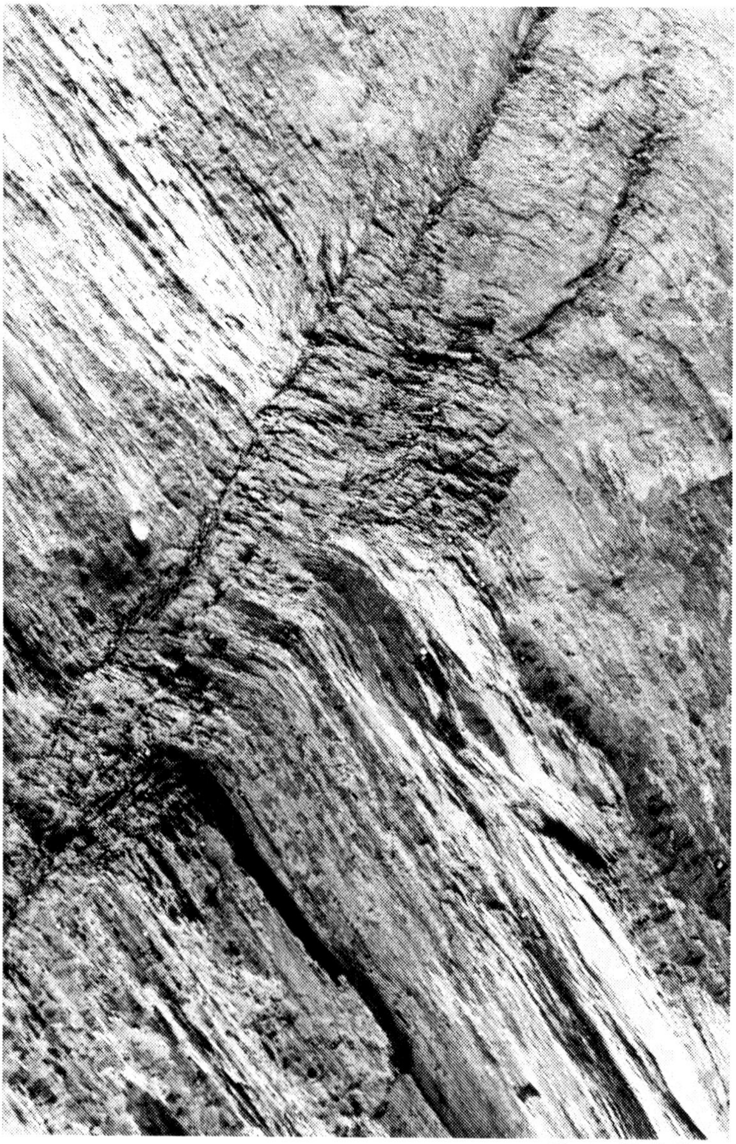

Photo: Neil Carter

Beyond and Here

There, just beyond the mist, Wales draws the mind over water's few jagged acres, attracts as these cloud-draped inland hills cannot. Even knowing that life over there will be much as here, still its seeming strangeness feeds the imagination, creates a yearning. Visible at times only as a lumpy blue horizon; in pre-rain clarity, when the grooves in its cliffs are clearly marked, mountain after mountain greenly recedes.

From the clifftop haunt of lark and vole, there,
in the fog-grey, one wave crest winks white; and,
out from under the haze, comes a long-winged
gannet,
whiter than foam or quartz, wing tips black
from skimming night's ink-dark waves.

Licensing laws have long changed, but still the Sunday trippers come across to get drunk. The young and simple, frantic with noise, announce their coming with tribal chants. Groups of young men, full of ale and a need for excitement, pound through these few streets. Bands pump their beat out over the harbour. Befuddled fat boys upheave themselves out of low pub seats. Holidaying girls - all clothes and earrings and no *joie de vivre* - scream their moment's inclusion.

Here and Beyond

The weather here is bigger than the people and their buildings. Could one aspire to be a hero here? Possibly. More likely in a city, where people see only their own window-reflected importance, or fight against the insignificance of their crowded sameness. Any such has to be plain foolish here, small between the moors and the changing sea.

Across a sea of wrinkles
a single cormorant goes
flying low, shadow black
as its under-mirror image.

Wales is
a land not always there
at day's horizon. Ghosting
behind mist, it exists more
in the mind. England
is a rumour inland.

Out of this substance of uncertainty, we, who have come here to die, want to tell you of the exquisiteness of all living things, as if they will be missed, seen no more by any other. Last spring, along the shattered cliffs, two grey-backed peregrines arrowed down at a black raven, which, twisting, turned talons up at each diving falcon. Writers are a people with no history, have to make their own.

"By means of poetry a man more rapidly approaches the cutting edge that the philosopher and the mathematician turn away from in silence."
Frederico Garcia Lorca

more than

In land and seascape replication of shapes
pythagorean triangles are reflected in flecks
of mica, flakes of shale and in the polished
pointed leaves of rock-rooted ivy. An offshore
wind scallops the sea, mirroring feathered
cirrus which, in turn, apes bracken fronds,
with the whole opaque sky in the milk-blank eye
of a cow. See how, up here, in moonlight,
below a bone-white rockface, where sheep
have grazed, galaxies of tiny saxifrage
star the grass. Watch the green frost growth
of gorse; until dawn is met by the klaxon
of a raven's croak. Pick your way down, under
this new pearled sky of unhewn marble, see
the mirror-twist, again, and again, of water. Note
how, within each curve of each smoothing wave,
lies all rocks' future roundness; while life's
defiance has a constellation of white limpets
stuck to a sun-dried, tilted slab of slate.

52 – apostrophe combe – Sam Smith, Gemma Dart and Neil Carter

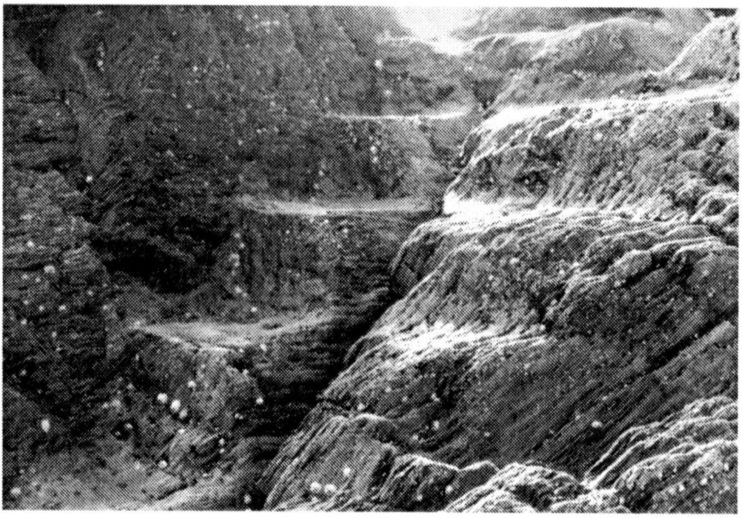

Photo: Neil Carter

'combe tanka

Beside a whitened sea
a cliff path of worn and ribbed rock:
jewelled flies crawl over
hogsweed floret domes;
and montbresias flame.

54 – apostrophe combe – Sam Smith, Gemma Dart and Neil Carter

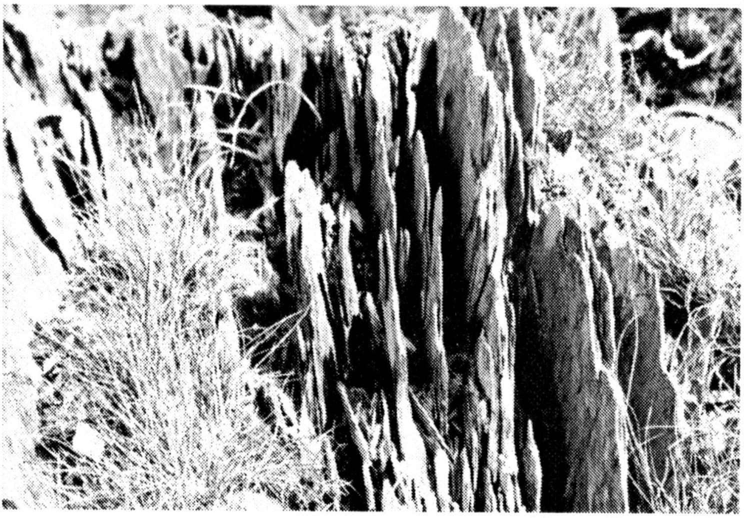

Photo: Gemma Dart

'combe haiku

This calm day has been
painted on glass, a line drawn
under Wales, bluely receding

56 – apostrophe combe – Sam Smith, Gemma Dart and Neil Carter

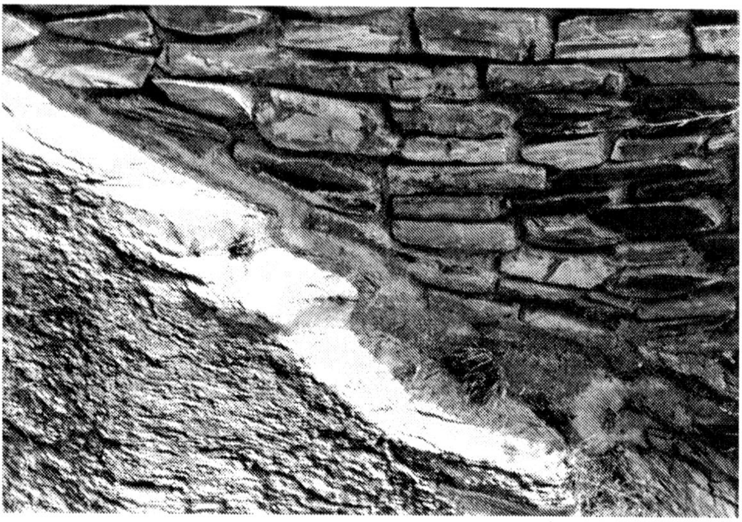

Photo: Gemma Dart

Larus Argentatus

With three white dots in the black of their folded back
wingtips, adult gulls are pristine in their spring
plumage,
eighteen years of cunning in their orange look.

This higgledy-piggledy rockface, infested with pink cave-dwelling apes, has chimney stack/rocky outcrops for perching and shitting on. Dazed chicks walk extension roofs, test tarry substances and surfaces with their black beaks; soon as fledged are taught to slit open plastic rubbish sacks and pull chip wrappers out of bins. In the sunken square of the tide-out harbour a few take slow turns to peel apart thrown-out dogfish and skate.

Early uncertainty gets many juvenilles killed;
and this every summer massacre, by cats and cars,
results in a lifetime's keening for the parents.

Some gulls, opening wide their yellow beaks, do try to sing; but their innate grief has them always off-key, and sticking on the one discord. Even when two or more try to string that one note together, their timing's always off. So they confine themselves to standing and, drawing their one call from between their web-ended legs, pointing an inflated gullet at the sky, they blare,

"Food!" or
"Foe!"

Flight calls, except for a yearling bleating after a parent, are quieter; and flying their true art. With three-dimensional maps in their heads, guided by a lexicon of gull murmur and an inner chart of air-flows, these clever, unafraid birds, whether walking or in flight, look always left to right, left to right. While, their artistry incomplete, just before rain they patter-dance their flat webbed feet on lawns and cropped pastures; headcocked knead this green world for worms.

Hunched together on the putting green, mottled grey-brown yearlings whimper out the storm. In the lull, within the cliff's arms of each cove, a grey-white gull, circling, inspects the new, the ever new.

Where the New Dumnonii Are

On the edge
of sea's cold distances
this town,
council neglected,
lives in its own shadow,
bits and parts
of its buildings gone
and going derelict;
subdivided and left
to those already dead,
no other heirs, nor
claimants,
and with always one
local tradesman
accruing such properties
and letting them
rot or for rent.
Year round
inhabitants walk
with their heads
down
- from the effort of
plodding up
the hills;
but also
to avoid
the dogshit.

They are a people
	here
	of a kind,
	but not sure
of their belonging,
	of their worth.

Perception Depends on Mood

(Similarly, without emotional content, logic can have no force.)

1) In town

Only with ale in their belly
can the English celebrate,
break through the silence
they day-by-day numb
themselves with. Self-centred,
dope-centred,
pub-centred existences,
reactionary and self-serving,
English through and through,
red white & blue, they
lay claim to a past that may
have produced them but
that existed without
any thought of them.

The large is in the small,
the small is in the large:
I keep myself remote here,
neither openly praise nor condemn,
lest I become part of their madness.

2) Out of town

Cream cloud has been piped and heaped upon an ink-blue horizon. Flat shadow islands re-pattern the sea, are punctuated here and there by the inverted white apostrophe of a yacht's sails. Dry soil is suspended in a web of roots over this cliff's edge. At cliff's base are triangular rocks like models of mountain ranges, their slab flat backs receding like so many wet lead roofs.

Breathing is difficult.

Edges 1

Railings of old footpaths bend, ending over cliff's edge. Part
foundations, with red & black tiled floor (gorse needles
drifting
into once corners), stop in a saw-toothed edge. Sections
of slid-off cliff have small twisted oaks clinging to their
slanted tops. On serrated rockfaces splodges of orange

form lines behind flat black lichen, curling white at its tips.
Rock's points claw at the sky and sunlight slides along
spider strands. The cloudscape is a scraping of blue, fat
cumulus floating within striated cirrus. One puffed out cloud
is reflected cream-fuzzy in the blue on blue shadowed sea.

In sheep pastures, among stamen halos of plantain
and thistle sentinels, ragged ewes use square mesh
fences, and redundant posts, to rub out their rear-end
underwool itches. Short-legged bullocks are boxed on
a field's horizon. Up there a gateway notch in a hedge.

Around woodland corners, above high walls and banks of
grey
slotted stone, are hidden houses with gardened ledges. Down
in the town, children - on the edge of trust - stand behind
their
parents, listening. Such converse as there is is on
the cusp of languages, borrowers and bastardisers all.

The young, not yet wholly sceptical, still prepared to do what they're told; they wait, watching for the word this day that will betray them. Outside the church, wearing suits, men meet for a funeral, greet each other by shaking hands, their shined faces twisted around grief yet to be expressed.

Edges 2

In this anxious old age, where things stay lost; and,
when found, unremembered; white-haired women,
wearing beige, link arms to go to the shops.
A tap coughs, hiss and splutter: an old man,
bending out of his chair, pauses to listen
to the gnat's whine of his tinnitus.
The bald woman twisted into the seat
opposite - no faith to take refuge in, no
certainty even of a definite
unknown, no assuredness of guessed-ats
- she worries around and about her pain,
a character all its own stabbing her
instantly alert; with, the rest of the time,
the waiting for the pain as debilitating
as the pain itself. A wanderer in
slippers wants to tell how important parts
of his life have been, dates that mattered; and
he doesn't recognise the freckles on
the back of his hand. And here, on the hard rim
of her bed, this one sits and weeps: divorce
and/or death, bereaved and bereft, at
memory's edge.

Here Henry Williamson Concocted Tarka the Otter along with His Very Own Brand of British Fascism

Singly, and in pairs, they come along these
narrow cliff paths, carbon-fibre walking staffs
in hand, pilgrims for pilgrimage sake. On
one cliff edge a man sits among gnat swarms
as dense as plankton; and, beside
sheep tearing at the grass, he stares
into the unfocused infinity of himself.

On the next grey outcrop stands a spinster, upright
and prickly as a thistle. Considerate walkers
pass by behind, heel-to-toe quietly, trying to
leave these two clifftop contemplatives undisturbed.

(I, a supposedly sensitive soul, tell you of this
with a poet's tired voice, wearisome delivery.
Those who wear sandals don't speak urgently
of scandals. Although, in denial of that, inside
this writer there is, of course, another writer
taking notes. And inside that writer there is...)

Way below are the brown, barnacle-softened,
outlines of tidal rocks. The freshly-fallen are
razor racked. In the driftline, down on that
shingle beach, will be the cliché of one
unlaced trainer and a split traffic cone.
On this day, an offshore wind flattens
the wave-frizzed sea in small rippled fans.

68 – apostrophe combe – Sam Smith, Gemma Dart and Neil Carter

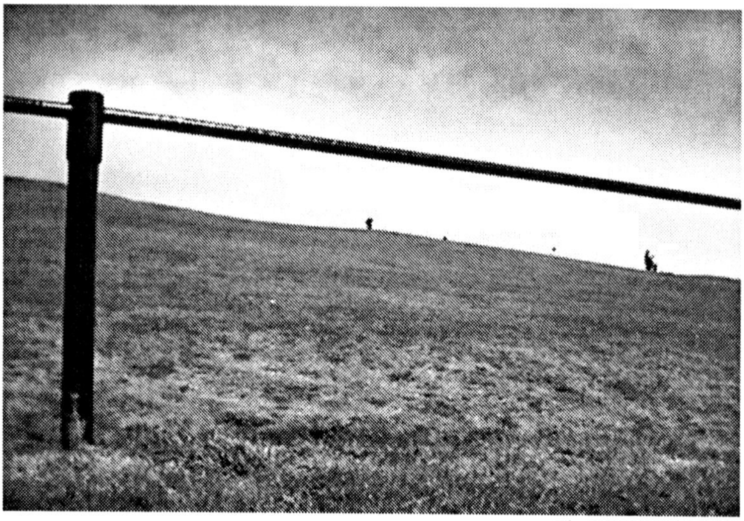

Photo: Neil Carter

the Hour 1

During the flour-dusted nights of bakers,
dog-piss graffiti on their outside walls, Wales
a poorly perforated line of orange dots and
Swansea's meringue smoke mauve-tinted;

to the nuzzling murmur of new lovers
just before sleep, two in the morning,
desperate to score, junkies come down
our street, banging on every door.

the Hour 2

One shout breaks into mushy night,
disperses in shards through
the white noise of cliff-base surf.

Nougat stratas of quartz waver
through rocks creased and wrinkled
like weathered hide, where land and
sea make a soggy cymbal crash.

Roadside echo-smells are of damp
rot. Acrid fumes, too, hang in the air:
a car was started here an hour ago.

Drizzle drifts down from the black hills,
gives each streetlight its own cone
of orange rain. A fox comes - out of
and into dark. Behind a window

a tongue-flattened cough; and through
the drumskin doors of a passing car
the heartbeat pulse of dance music.

'combe tanka

Atop a wall of slotted stone
red-berried cotoneaster creeps up over
cemented-in pebbles of quartz.
Earth's waters rise to the magnet
of a cloud-smudged moon.

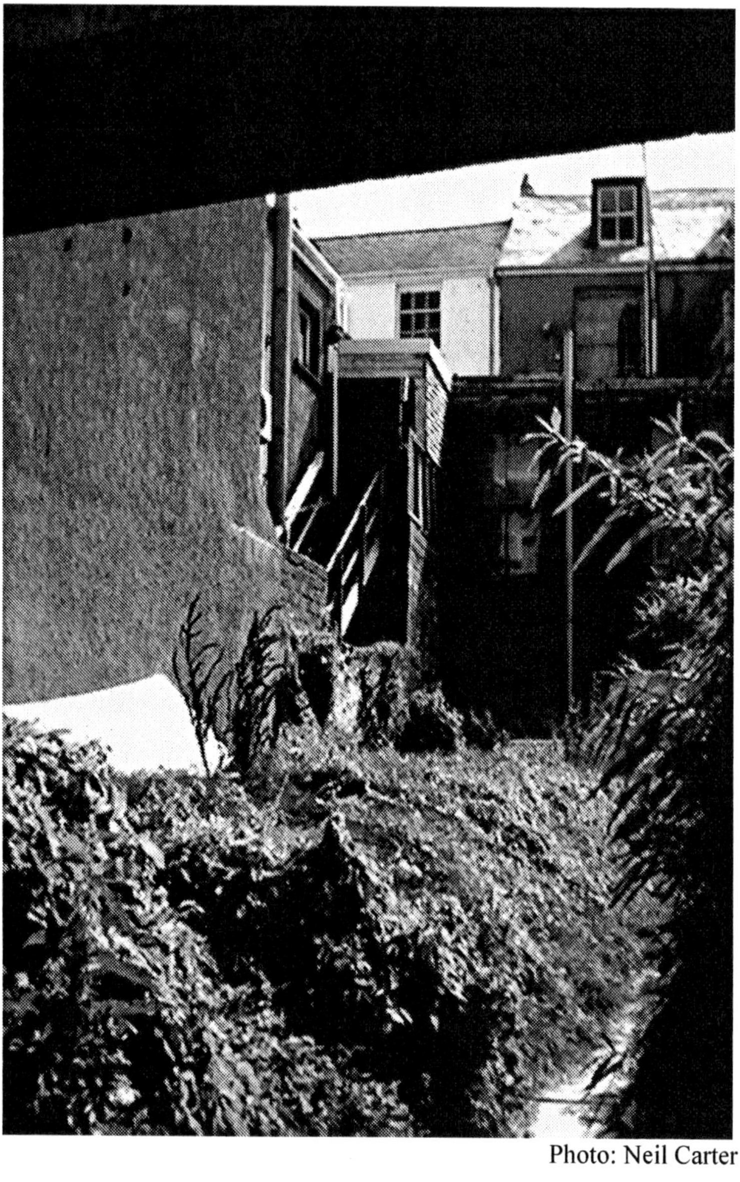

Photo: Neil Carter

'combe haiku

a window traffic
of gulls: we own the comfort
and tyranny of routines

the opposite of tunnel vision

Bodies, arranged in stone-baked nooks, are being inspected by the compound eyes of ornate dragonflies. Over the slow wave-snoring sea and the trickling creep of the tide can be heard the waft of white butterfly wings and the occasional squeak of a rock pippet. A squadron of oyster-catchers, with one commanding shriek, arrows around the coast.

> Next headland along is a rack of rock
> grey doors, part slewed, part capsized,
> then pushed back, broken, collapsed and
> restored again. Painful memories clack
> together like hand-cupped pebbles.

Properties of light and water mean that sky cannot reflect sea. Although the sea's maggot wriggle of microbes does serve to augment sky's colours; the surface, by its reflection, emphasising the pinky gold of the clouds and appearing to deepen the blue. This September day, with a prolonged dog-sleep groan, an orange boat chalks a wake across band after band of blue metal light.

In our Steep Street

In our steep street the tall houses are divided into flats. The doorbells to the flats do not work. Visitors to the flats stand in the middle of the street and moo. People living in the flats occasionally appear at a window. On recognising a caller they may come down the many stairs to open the street door. Or, more likely, they quickly retreat from their window. The people in the street will continue to moo.

The farmer leaves his four-by-four in the carpark at the top of our steep street. The farmer is self-conscious in his coming-to-town clothes. He walks looking down at his clean shoes, looks up with every other long step, looks down at his clean shoes. His wife hurries to catch up. She is dressed in her farmer's wife clothes, bought from the farmer's wife clothes shop, which is next to the farmer's wife hairdressers.

At the top of our steep street they stop at sight of all the people mooing. The dogs have been left back at the farm. The farmer and his wife turn around, leave the carpark by another exit.

Rusty

sent to fetch the dog
the girl stands
just outside her door.
"Rusty!"
she calls once,
waits.

"Rusty!"
she calls again,
waits.

"Rusty!"
her torso
sinks into
her hips.

"Rusty!"
Her mouth is
opening
to the rhythm
of her breathing.

"Rusty!"
Both name
and action
are coming
to lose
meaning.

"Rusty!"
The intent
forgotten
she has gotten
locked into,

"Rusty!"
the sound
of herself
making
the sound,

"Rusty!"

Being Within the Passage of Time...

...into the grey evening, into the wind gullies of the empty streets, come stilted twelve year olds. Daring to be daring, desperately wanting to be notorious, they make noise. To do so they need to be together, these budding young with their catch-all irreverence, for death even. Yet innocent still of love's many aspects and conjunctions, their faces planed naked, they make plans that take them nowhere but to the all-year-round arcade, where the usual winners and losers are locked into their machines, ears cocked for who is feeding what other machine, for - above the come-on jingles - the percussive rattle of a win. Later comes the sick anger when these grown men and women have blown a week's wages on the electronically prompted pressing of buttons. Meanwhile - in among fussing mothers, besotted by their own infants - the growing young practise the smoking of cigarettes, the swearing out loud and the spitting. The girls have shiny shaved shins. One short-skirted girl has a blue bruise on her white calf, mappings of mauve capillaries on her round thighs. One slight girl's rapid laughter is aimed at a passing other's back. Another, her mind gripped by the anchor roots of anxiety, her mouth set in soon-to-be perpetual misery, wearing now a mask of herself, she walks through unpeopled spaces as lonely as a ship at sea. Later, as this evening's dramas develop, as new alliances are formed, all building up to the deliberated-on brutality of country boys to anyone not presently of their tribe; these brief episodes, within their final period of growth, will become fixed in their memory's eternity. With, all the while, in the same darkened corner, one enwrapped pair nuzzling and stroking with the slow, so slow, self-absorption of sensuality. They will relinquish one the other in a daze...

whimsy

this present
this here and now
is infinite
has always been and will always be

beyond this sea's edge
skies of marshmallow wonder
clouds of all varieties
and all in pastel shades

Here
is the evening chill
that comes off calm water

Here
on this harbourside's square paving
sea-damp has made circles
around stray pebbles

Here
on a public seat a young woman
cardigan loose around her shoulders,
remembering a small pleasure,
lowers her head over a smile

Here
has always been and will always be

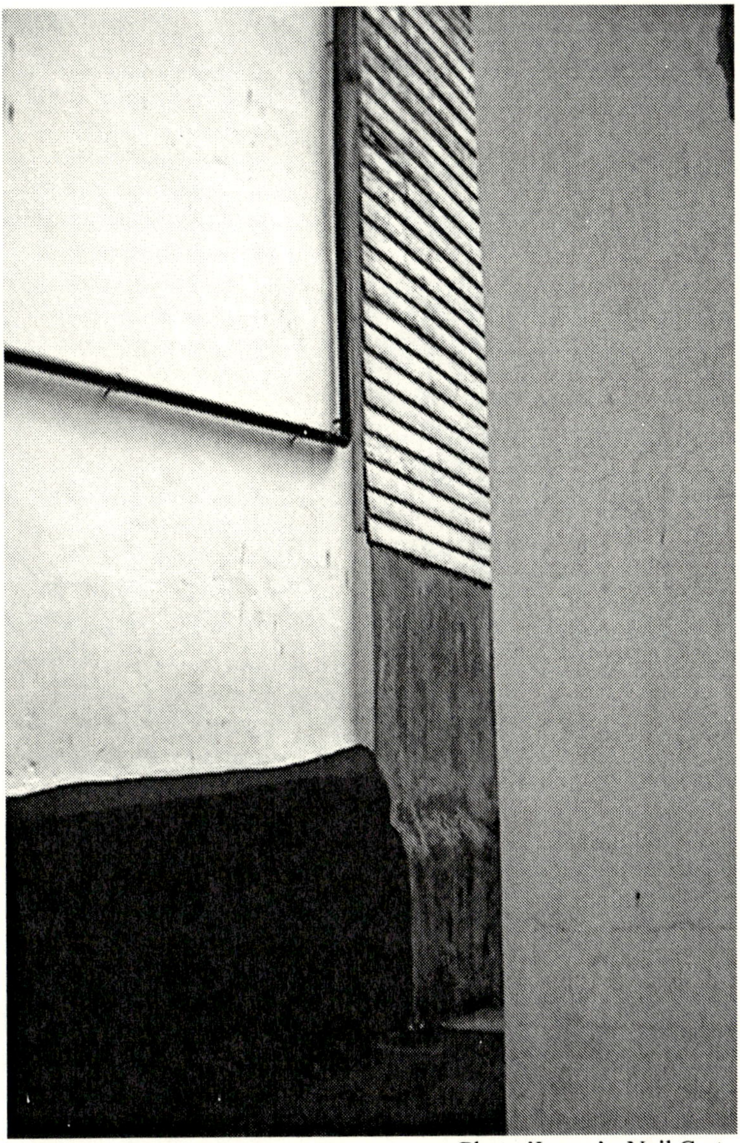

Photo:'Lanes' - Neil Carter

'combe tanka

Beside every scaffolded
renovation, next door slips a broken pane
further into dereliction.
Earth's shadow, at day's end,
rises up pinked Eastern clouds.

Defiance & Failure

Rank upon rank of slanted rocks Seig Heil the sea, a pewter sheen upon the silvered slabs of their cracked and adze-hewn backs. No illusions here, though, of rocks' solidity: all is being formed, unformed. Locals even take a delight in nature's destructive powers, the impersonal might of each new breaker; in the wind working on rattles to loosen them, and biting slates from roofs, shale from rockslide scree. Every small victory for the wind and sea, though, every new piece of cliff battered to the beach, becomes a new obstacle to the devouring waves. If temporary.

> Prisons come in many forms - jobs,
> routines, houses, families, partners,
> rituals. The mist defines the limits
> of here, barbarity but a scratch away.
> Fuschias blood both roads and pavements.

Here, in this lipservice culture, eyes still look to which flag is blowing which way in which wind. All businesses here sail close to bankruptcy - farms, pubs, restaurants, tourist shops - one wet summer, one piece of bad luck, creditors a week away, and all quickly comes unstuck. Even the young here have the haunted look of old men, glance anxiously about. The old men wait for the unremembered past to catch up with them, the young for something vital overlooked.

He Was A Good But Brutal Man

Breathing the cool shaded air - in the L of the cliff
and a beach of milk-teeth pebbles - he stands
dressed only in his skin and the idea of himself.
Beyond islands of pointed slate, passing over
an indigo, cloud-marbled sea, goes the floating
wall of an orange ship, cargo unguessed-at.

Green sea lettuce bewings low tidal rocks. Jelly knob-end
anenomes are, crimson, closed. The orange beak
of an oyster-catcher probes the cracks and crevices
of barnacle-brown triangular rocks. Tidal pools
are mirror shards. At cliff's grey-black base
salt-bleached spars are arranged in hexagrams.

He, himself, has been the prophet and experiment
of his life. Pointed at him incuriously now is a seal's
anvil head. Soft-eyed sea's deer, a sleek dappled fawn,
slippery as weed; it disappears in a blink. Standing
there, breathing the cool shaded air, dressed only
in his body of scars and unremembered wounds,

done with this vicious world of men, empty as
a tilted hulk in a cove, stripped of all parts
of any use to anyone, transparent to himself,
he waits to be washed apart by storm, time and tide.

Habits New

This fag smoke and spit platoon is a generation
grown up in noise - within earphones, clubs, arcades, traffic.
They communicate by hand signals, shouted slogans,
grimaces, a patina of cynicism,
a catechism of cued responses consciously
accrued to avoid being laughed at as naifs.
A high-breasted girl minces by in trainers.
The arcade hero wears a fag in the corner
of his mouth. The fluffy blonde on the gaming machine,
buttocks pouchy in tight trousers, smiles with her mouth
closed, as if she still has a brace. The smile is not
a happy smirk, rather she holds the top lip rigid,
allowing the lower to curl up around it. All
that money spent on her teeth, and now, out of habit,
she won't show them; not even in the instant,
enthusiastic friendships of the young, of an age
when they think it important to have an opinion
about every new pop song. In front of a window
wall of green lawn, upright youths on their skateboards
glide down the uneven pavements of Wilder Road,
one after the other...

'combe haiku

candle-yellow of gorse
glows among the smoky white
of blackthorn in bloom

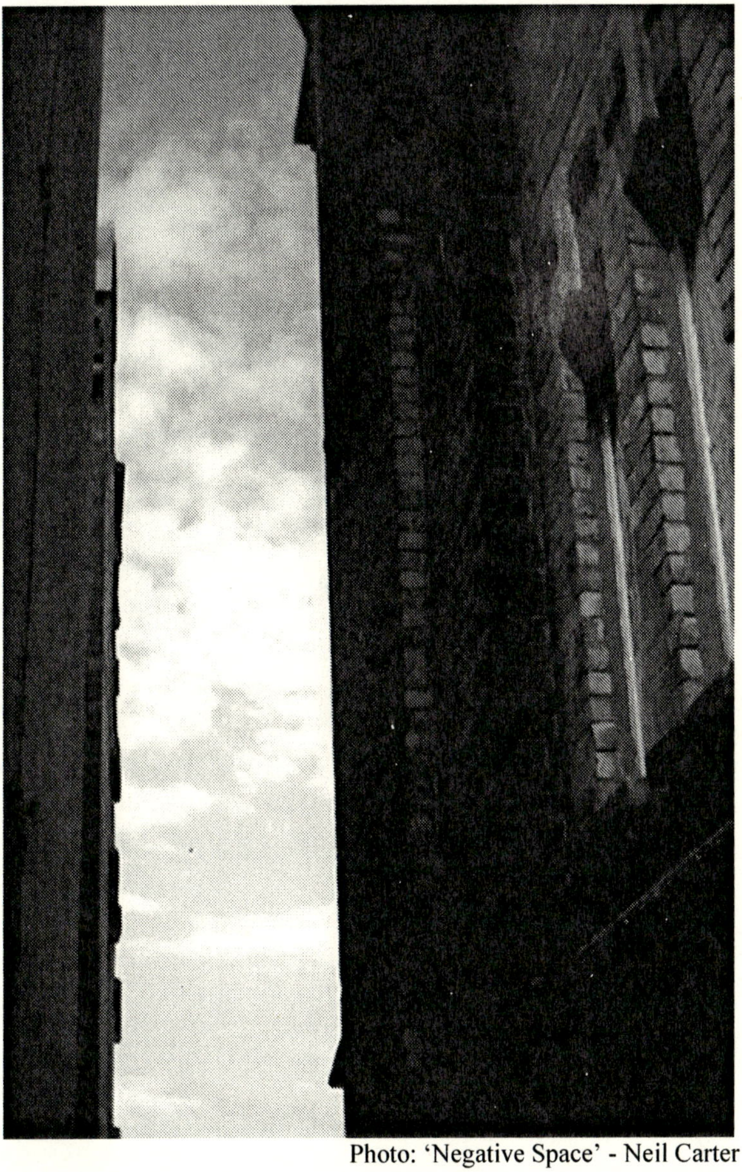

Photo: ‘Negative Space’ - Neil Carter

'combe tanka

A raft of gulls preen on
the reservoir's fresh water: beyond
the still day haze, fighter planes
roar and growl: fuschia
blooms bruise the ground.

their majesties

Over and above rock's grey co-ordinates,
black crosses marking out horizon's graph,
a pair of ravens make shadows one of
the other; and, keeping their distance, wait
on me (my heavy-beaked brethren, my
        ultimate friends, my skin-diggers,
        flesh-peelers, carcass-pickers, bone-
        scrapers; ready, at the fixing of an eye,
        to begin the process of my re-absorption.)

Imperturbably patient, crag-perched, these ravens
anticipate my death. In amongst their black-on-black
plumage, the same fixed smirk as a digesting snake.

This pair, with cautioning croaks, now shepherd their brood
of four above the off-white smudges of clifftop sheep and
in and around the stumps of upended and broken off strata.

I climb to the slab layered top and out to the edge;
and, of a sudden, in a pre-death visit, six ravens
are flying close, above, around, and below me; and
all six are growling and muttering back at my own
back-of-the-throat croaking; and, arms outstretched,
turning, fingertips to wingtips, in this laughing
laughing moment
I am immortal.

Switch on the Atrocity News? Or Not?

Down in the carpark a fat man's car leans to one side. Paper, from the recycling skip, has been trapped under black tyres. White plastic carrierbags are stuck to puddles. Two gulls patrol on a diagonal. Schoolchildren, hands free, are followed by their mothers, carrying bags. Let off its extendible leash, a black dog bounces back and forth with happiness, pausing to crouch and wag, bark once and bounce away again. Drivers, newly arrived, stand and stare at the charges board. It will be used later as a target by boys practising football.

> Between the rock's mouth
> a single white sail sits tall
> on today's indigo horizon:
> above summer's leaf-filled cushions of trees
> swifts go twinkling darkly up green combes.

That dogshit, which has been picked up in inside-out bags, reversed, there being no rubbish bins, has been chucked into the hedge. Two boys go into the swingpark through a gap in the hedge, rather than via the nearer gate. The wobbly-legged alcoholic gets pulled back by his rottweiller to every last smell. Three skinny skateboarders arrange a too thin length of wood as a pavement ramp, too close to a car. (The fascination here is of watching stupidity unfolding, of anticipating the probable consequences of poorly considered actions.) When clouds come down the combes, mountains can be imagined within them, up above the steep, mist-speckled fields and woods.

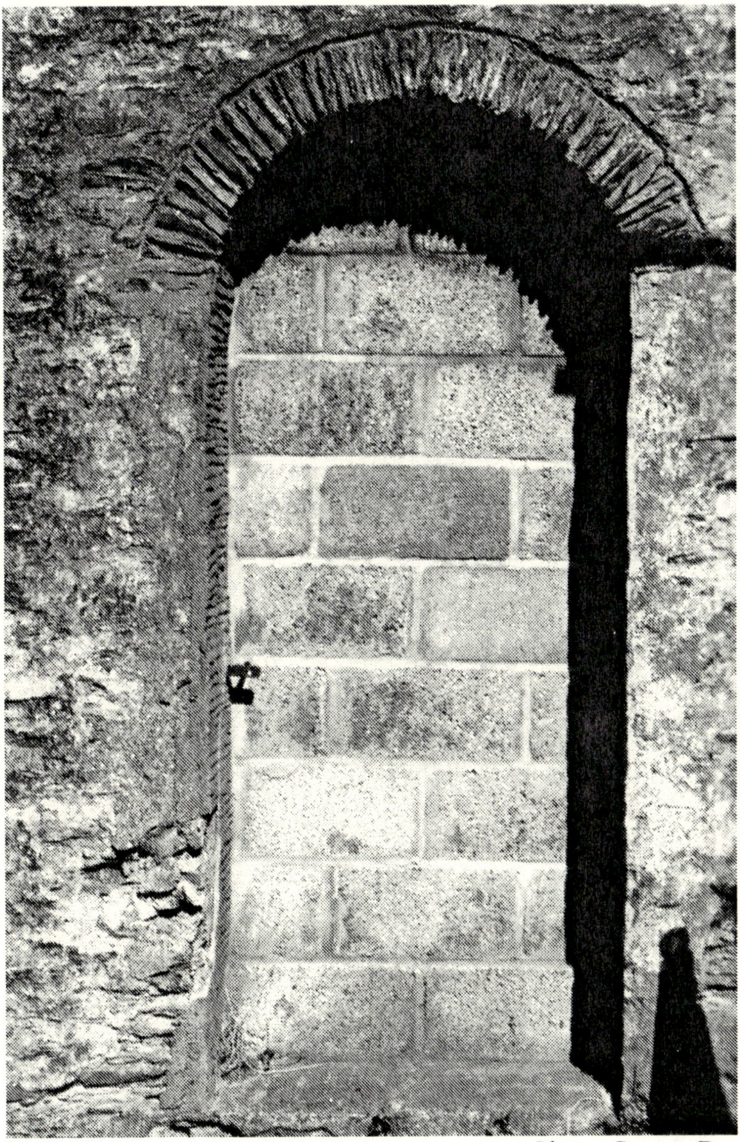

Photo: Gemma Dart

'combe tanka

Above the green wave of the hills
advancing to the sea, a translucent
half-moon floats tilted in
today's sky: on the beach a listed
hulk has been battered blue & red.

'combe haiku

thread-legged craneflies
rise out of the dense grass
before each footfall

Forgive me.

In the mythology of 'combe the mythologiser also has to be a self-invention.

[Glossy prints of any of the photographs here can be obtained by contacting Gemma Dart - gemmadart@hotmail.com]

previous publications by sam smith

novels

'Sister Blister' Online Originals 1999 ISBN 1 8404 047 9
'The End of Science Fiction' Jacobyte Books 2000 ISBN 174053028
'Paths of Error: Undeclared War' Jacobyte Books 2001 ISBN 174053073 X
'Paths of Error: Constant Change' Jacobyte Books 2001 ISBN 1740530780
'Paths of Error: As Recorded' Jacobyte Books 2002 ISBN 174100079-3
'Marks' 2002 BeWrite Books ISBN 1-904224-09-1
'Porlock Counterpoint' 2002 BeWrite Books ISBN 1-904224-15-6
'Care Vortex' 2002 BeWrite Books ISBN 1-904224-98-9
'Sick Ape: an everyday tale of terrorist folk' 2003 BeWrite Books ISBN 1-904492-15-0

non-fiction

'Vera & Eddy's War' BeWrite Books 2002 ISBN 1-904224-97-0

poetry collections

'To Be Like John Clare' University of Salzburg Press 1997 ISBN 3 7052 0066 6
'Skin&Bones' Odyssey Poets 1997 ISBN 1 897654 03 3
'Dialogues' Silver Gull Publishing 1998 ISBN 0 9527668 3 3
'John the Explorer' Gecko Press 1999 ISBN 0 9535844 0 2
'pieces' K.T.Publications 2001 ISBN 0907759432
'Rooms' Oasis Books 2003 ISBN 1 900996 27 8
'apostrophe combe' boho press 2003 ISBN 1-904781-02-0

Sam Smith is also the founding editor of 'The Journal of Contemporary Ango-Scandinavian Poetry', now known as 'The Journal'; is Poetry Editor of Jacobyte Books (Australia), British liaison for 'The River King Poetry Supplement' (USA);and is publisher of Original Plus books.

Original Plus titles

'Andetsteds' Don Ammons ISBN 0 9533591 0 7
'Other Moments' R G Bishop ISBN 0 9533591 2 3
'Other Places' Idris Caffrey ISBN 0 9533591 1 5
'Eeeny Minnie Molly' Richard Wonnacott ISBN 09533591 3 1
'Forgeries' James Turner ISBN 095335914X
'Bags of Mostly Water' Sandra Tappenden ISBN 0953359158
'Underland' Paul Davidson ISBN 0953359166
'Broadsheet Asphyxia' Paul Sutton ISBN 0953359174

apostrophe combe - 101

102 – apostrophe combe – Sam Smith, Gemma Dart and Neil Carter

bluechrome boho press

As you can see from the following pages, in the year since we launched bluechrome, we have managed to get together some of the finest authors and poets around and produced some exciting and at times strange fiction, alongside becoming what many see as a very real contender in the poetry world.

But what is new? Well, in November 2003, we will be formally launching a new imprint "**the boho press**", that will provide us with a greater flexibility of choice in what we publish in the coming years. The boho press is a little different from bluechrome, as we see it as much as a way of combating the vanity trade as anything else. Aiming at providing a way for writing groups or groups of writers to publish high quality anthologies, it gives us the opportunity to be a lot more flexible.

The best example of this is our collection of women's poets, *boho women peeling oranges*. For this we recognised the quality of the poetry that had been submitted to our annual competition and decided we'd like to do an additional collection. This happened in September and the collection will be available in time for Christmas, so if you'd like to see what all the fuss has been about, why not treat yourself to a copy.

If poetry is your thing, we also have the *2004 bluechrome anthology*, which represents the cream of the small press poetry scene in the UK today. This features the winners and short-list from our annual competition and has an additional bonus of selected poems from Gary Bills, Ronnie Goodyer, Geoff Stevens, Sam Smith and Les Merton – all of whom will have collections released over the coming months. Geoff and Gary's collection are also available in December of this year and are quite simply stunning.

On the fiction side, the Booker nominated *Nicolo's Gifts* is an obvious choice, but *Doctor Mooze* and the soon to be released *boys, Bedouins and castratos* are something completely different. Pulp.Net made *Doctor Mooze* their book of the month ahead of people like Douglas Coupland, and *bB&c*, our first joint release in conjunction with "The Burning Book Press", shows a kind of talent little seen since the demise of the *Beat* Generation.

All in all, 2003 has been a fantastic year and we are proud to have been able to work with some great authors and poets, and I would like to thank you for your support.

Kind Regards

Anthony Delgrado

October 2003

bluechrome fiction

Doctor Mooze – Panton di Villa

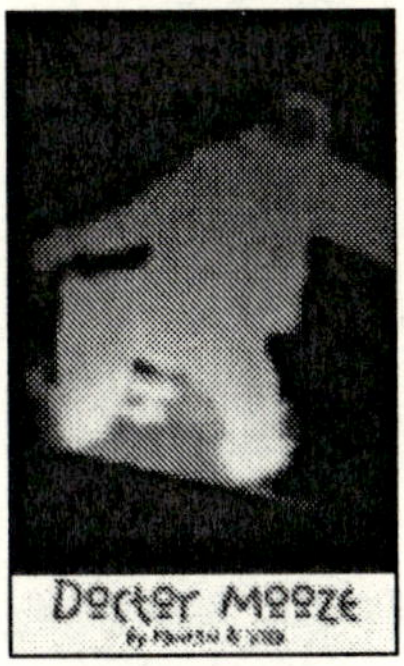

Panton di Villa was a Ten-Year-old boy who wanted to write a Blog like all his mates at school - but really couldn't be bothered to find out how. Instead he thought he'd get the diary he wrote over Christmas released as a book. In this modern Catcher in the Rye, Panton gives an insight into what it is really like to be an adolescent boy in England today - definitely not one for the kids. Pulp.Net made it their "new Book of the Month" and said "*For sheer everyday weirdness of the kind that rarely makes it to print, it's book of the month on Pulp Net, and hang the Booker nominations.*"

Nicolo's Gifts – Neil Ayres

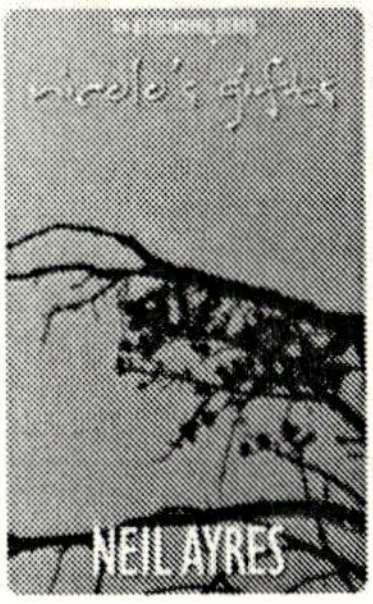

Nicolo's Gifts is as honest an exploration of the human condition as you are likely to find. Literature, folktales and the constant struggle of the astute mind against the mundane are fused with audacity. Prepare to be enraptured by characters that are as wise as they are naïve and as beatific as they are flawed. Textured and tiered tales at once intriguing and astounding await the adventurous reader. This novel is a genre-blending paradox to delight those of a more exploratory nature.

bluechrome poetry

The Phrenology of Anaglypta – Geoff Stevens

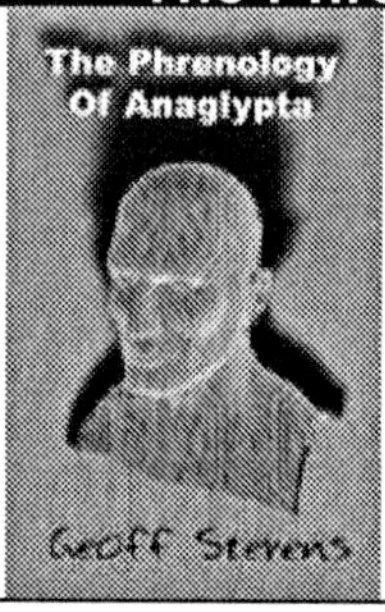

Funny, irreverent, touching and of the highest quality, the Phrenology of Anaglypta showcases the talents of one of those rare people who can turn diversity into an art form in itself

Bluechrome 2004 Anthology – Editor Ronnie Goodyer

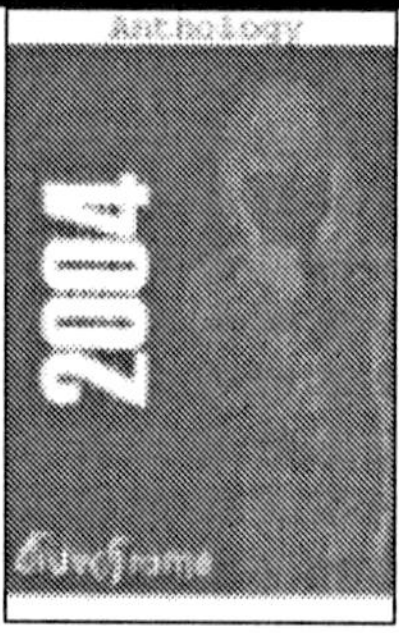

This year's anthology is exclusively poetry, and includes the winners and short-listed entries from the annual bluechrome poetry competition. Additionally, we have the special bonus of some of bluechrome's best-known poets chipping in a couple of their finest pieces of work. Ronnie Goodyer, Gary Bills, Sam Smith, Geoff Stevens and Les Merton all join our 2004 Poet of the Year, Helen Kitson, in this stunning collection

bluechrome

bluechrome,
PO Box 109
Portishead
Bristol
BS20 7ZJ

To order, please complete the form and forward it to the above address enclosing a cheque for the full amount in **£sterling**, made payable to "bluechrome publishing".

Title	Price	Quantity	Cost
Doctor Mooze	£7.99		
Nicolo's Gifts	£7.99		
Indigo Dreams	£7.99		
Seven Sweet Things	£10.00		
Ridiculous Nests of the Heart	£7.99		
The Phrenology of Anaglypta	£7.99		
Bluechrome 2004 Anthology	£7.99		
boys, Bedouins and castratos	£10.00		
Voices from the Web	£12.99		
The Rainbow Man	£7.99		
Apostrophe Combe	£7.99		
boho women peeling oranges	£7.99		

Total:			
P&P:			£2.50
Grand Total:			

Printed in the United Kingdom
by Lightning Source UK Ltd.
108858UKS00001B/12

9 781904 781028